I want a Dog

W

FRANKLIN WATTS
LONDON • SYDNEY

My name is Alex and I've always wanted a dog more than anything else in the world. Mum and Dad are not so keen though. Nor is the rest of my family! They all have a reason why they don't want a dog.

Aren't dogs very messy? They can poo and wee inside and damage the furniture.

You'll get bored with the dog and then I'll have to walk it!

A dog will jump up and make my clothes muddy.

But my friends have dogs and they aren't messy, scary or boring. I've decided to make this scrapbook all about dogs. I'll show the different breeds of dogs, what they are like and how to look after them. I'm going to prove to

Rescue Centre

Body Language

Vet Advice

Dogs can be scary. They bark and scare me sometimes.

Where will it sleep? This house isn't big enough for both of us.

Today is the last day of school. Hurrah! To celebrate, some of my classmates have brought in their dogs for Show and Tell. There is a Staffordshire Bull Terrier, a Pug and a Siberian Husky. We all get a chance to stroke the dogs and ask about their care.

Today my friend Ruby and I are walking her dog, Jack, who is a well-trained Labrador.

At a road Ruby's mum tells Jack to sit. We all wait until the cars have passed and we can cross.

When we get to the park Ruby says, "Come on, you can take his lead now. Don't worry, it's easy and I'll tell you what to do."

Jack might try and pull you along. If he tugs on the lead, stop walking. That shows him that pulling makes you stop, not go forward.

On the way home Ruby asks me if I would like to do this every day with my dog. I can't think of anything better.

My dad is pleased I have tried out dog walking. As a treat, he takes us to a dog show in the park. Here, there are dozens of different dogs taking part. Some are performing tricks and others are in competitions. My sister Amy takes photos of my favourite dogs.

The winner of the obedience competition is a clever Border Collie. His owner says people should choose a dog that will fit with their family life and home. "Border Collies were bred as farm dogs and need lots of exercise," he says.

No, we've taught him not to do that.

We all have a brilliant day at the dog show. Even Amy likes the dogs and we all laugh and learn a lot.

This Afghan Hound had a long coat and loved chasing things. His owner said he needed lots of grooming.

This Pointer was very friendly and had an amazing nose. He could smell the crisps in my pocket straight away!

This Pomeranian loved to play and had a high-pitched bark we could hear all over the park.

We learned a lot about dog breeds at the show. Each breed belongs to one of seven groups. I found some pictures of one member from each group for my scrapbook. Some of them reminded me of dogs I saw at the show.

HOUNDS

w h o o s h

Hounds were bred to hunt, so they like to chase things. This Greyhound was friendly and very fast.

TERRIERS

Terriers were bred to catch rats and rabbits. This Scottish Terrier was small but he wasn't scared of anything!

UTILITY DOGS

There are lots of different dogs in the Utility group, but mostly they are kept as pets. This Poodle seemed clever and caring.

WORKING DOGS

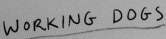

Working dogs ... help people, such as rescuing them from beneath the snow like this St Bernard. The St. Bernard was gigantic but gentle.

Sheepdog ... farm animals. The she... energetic with loads of hair.

GUNDOGS

Gundogs like this English Springer Spaniel were bred to help hunters. The Springer Spaniel was keen to play with us.

TOY DOGS

Toy dogs are little dogs bred to keep people company. This Pug was friendly and loved us patting him.

On Sunday we visit my gran and her dog Ruffles. Ruffles is a Jack Russell Terrier that Gran got from a rescue centre. Gran says Ruffles is a proud little dog with a big personality.

Gran says a house needs to be dog-proofed before a dog is brought home for the first time. Gran's cat Lucy also came from a rescue centre. Gran made sure that Ruffles left Lucy alone.

No. He was an adult when I got him and already housetrained.

Gran made lots of special hiding places for Lucy. Lucy escapes to these places if she gets sick of Ruffles.

Ruffles had his own bed in Gran's Laundry room. It was a strong basket with a big cushion and blanket inside.

Ruffles loves to explore and Gran keeps dangerous things out of reach. These include electrical cords and small things that he could choke on.

Ruffles

After visiting Gran, my mum asks how we could make our house ready for a dog. We walk around together, looking for a place where he could sleep and eat. Then we talk about 'dog-proofing' our home.

I show Mum a quiet, warm corner in our kitchen away from the noisy dishwasher and washing machine. This would be perfect for a dog's food and water bowls. We find another place for a bed.

After Dad fixes the holes in the fence, we have a safe garden for a dog to play and go to the toilet in. Mum says we could clear some high shelves on our bookcases for our cat Tigger to escape from a dog.

Gran gave me this shopping list

Shopping List for new dog

Tough, rubber toys that a dog can chew on but are too big to swallow.

A collar with an ID tag and a lead for walks.

Bowls with rubber rims so they don't get pushed around. Dogs need fresh water every day.

Child locks for low cupboards (this stops a dog opening them and hurting himself).

Gran X

Mum says we have the space for a dog, but she is still not sure about getting one. She worries a dog may be badly behaved and damage the furniture. I tell her that dogs can be taught to behave well. To convince my mum, we visit a dog training session.

There are lots of dogs at the training session: puppies, adults, pure-bred dogs, cross-bred dogs and mongrels. The trainer is helping the dog owners to teach their dogs good behaviour.

Today my dad and I take Tigger for her vaccination injections at the vet's. The vet's waiting room is an interesting place with lots of different dogs. Most of the dogs seem calm, but one has his tail tucked between his legs and is trembling. He looks scared.

After Tigger gets her injections, the vet tells us that dogs need vaccination injections too. These protect against disease and mean that they can meet other dogs outside the home.

Visiting the vet's makes some pets nervous. The best thing is to talk to them in a soothing voice and stay calm.

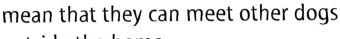

ADVICE FROM THE VET

VACCINATION

 Puppies need vaccination injections between 6 and 16 weeks of age. They should not meet other animals outside the house until after their last injection.

A vet can talk with owners about having their dog neutered, which stops them having puppies.

MICRO CHIPPING

All dogs need to have a microchip inserted beneath their skin, which is painless. The microchip contains a dog's details in case he gets lost.

Caring for your new dog

GROOMING

Dog owners need to regularly brush their dog's coat to keep it clean and untangled.

At home, I tell my sister Katie about the scared dog at the vet's. "How did you know he was scared?" Katie asks. To explain, I show her some pictures about dog body language.

The vet gave me a poster about dog body language for my scrapbook. Dogs use three main 'poses' to show us how they feel. These are scared, happy and angry.

BODY LANGUAGE

He is ready to...

SCARED
This dog shows he is scared by tucking his tail between his legs, flattening his ears and trying to look small. You can help a scared dog to relax by not looking at them, giving them lots of space and talking in a calm voice.

ANGRY
This angry dog has his tail in the air, his ears pointing forwards and is showing his teeth. This dog is saying, "Go away!" and it is best to walk away quietly and leave him alone.

Alex

A few weeks ago our neighbour Jayden had exciting news. His parents are Boxer breeders and one of their dogs gave birth to a litter of puppies. Now, the puppies are ready to be introduced to new people. My sisters and I rush around at once.

Jayden's parents are Kennel Club Assured Scheme breeders and so Jayden has grown up around lots of puppies. He says puppies need to get used to new people and animals so they grow into confident adults. This is called 'socialisation'.

This one was my favourite puppy. He was very adventurous.

Puppies should get used to as many different people and animals as possible before they reach 14 weeks of age.

Puppies also need to get used to new noises. Jayden played his puppies recordings of cars, buses and lawn mowers from the internet. This means they won't be scared of the noises when they go outside.

Puppies need to go to the toilet every 1-2 hours and should be taken to the same spot in the garden to become housetrained. Jayden also took the puppies into the garden after food, naps and first thing in the morning.

Dad has organised something special for us today. He is taking us to a rescue centre to visit the dogs there. The rescue centre looks after dogs who don't have an owner. Some of the dogs look lonely. Dogs are like us – they need a home and people to look after them!

Jenny shows us around. She says that the rescue centre finds homes for thousands of dogs. Their dogs are a mixture of pure-breeds, cross-breeds and mongrels. Pure-bred dogs have parents of the same breed, but Jenny says this does not make them better pets. "All dogs can make great pets. It doesn't matter who their parents are," she says.

Finally it is time to leave. It's been a great day and Jenny has given me loads of advice for my scrapbook.

JENNY'S ADVICE

Never shout at a dog if ...thing wrong

Be careful where you get a dog from. Rescue centres and Kennel Club Assured Scheme breeders are best.

Adult dogs make just as good pets as puppies. Often they have already been trained, too.

Taking a rescue dog is a wonderful way of giving a dog a new life.

Today is the greatest day of my life! It began when my family told me how much they enjoyed my scrapbook. They said all of my work had helped them like and understand dogs. My scrapbook is a success! I've never been so pleased and proud.

New dog owners need help to care for their dog. Here's some helpful advice from my scrapbook that every dog owner should know.

Dogs don't like to be left alone. Somebody needs to be at home to keep them company.

Dogs need to be walked every day, even if it's raining, snowing or there's something great on TV.

w h o o s h

Dogs can live with other pets, but they both need their own spaces and to be introduced to each other properly.

There are loads of different dogs and it's important to choose one that will fit in with your family life and home. Dogs with lots of energy may not suit small homes without any outside space.

Dogs learn by having their good behaviour rewarded and their bad behaviour ignored.

A home must be dog-proofed to make it safe before a dog comes home for the first time.

Dogs show us if they are happy, angry or scared through their body language.

Be careful where you get a dog from. Rescue centres and Kennel Club Assured Scheme breeders are best.

Puppies need to be socialised with as many different people, animals and sounds as possible before 14 weeks of age.

Throw the bird! Throw the bird! Throw the bird!

Bringing up a dog is great fun but can also be a lot of work. Make sure everyone in your home is happy to help before you get one!

BATTERSEA DOGS & CATS HOME

Battersea dogs & cats home is a famous rescue centre which looks after 5,000 dogs and 3,500 cats every year. Battersea has centres in London, Berkshire and Kent that never turn away a dog or cat in need. Over 1,000 volunteers, carers and veterinary staff look after the animals and help find them new homes.

Visit the website at: battersea.org.uk

INSURANCE

Pet insurance is recommended to cover the cost of vet bills. Visit the Battersea website for more information.

DOG IDENTIFICATION

By law dogs have to be microchipped and wear a collar and ID tag in public. The ID tag must have your surname, telephone number and address on it. Visit the Battersea website for more information about microchipping.

Lennon
297 Lincoln Road
Cheshire
06592 111322

GLOSSARY

CROSS-BREED
A dog bred from two
different breeds.

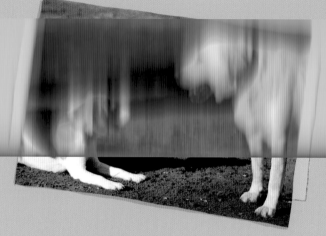

HOUSE-TRAINED
Trained to go to the toilet
outside of the house.

LITTER
A number of young animals
born at the same time to
one parent. There are usually
between three and eight
puppies in a dog litter.

MICROCHIPPED
Inserting a small microchip
with the owner's details into
the scruff of a dog's neck.

MONGREL
A dog bred from parents
of multiple breeds.

NEUTERING
An operation which stops an
animal from having babies.

PURE-BREED
A dog bred from parents of
the same breed.

RESCUE CENTRE
A place that takes stray
or unwanted pets and finds
them new homes.

VACCINATION
A treatment to protect
against disease.

Franklin Watts
First published in Great Britain in 2017
by The Watts Publishing Group

Illustrations copyright © Jason Chapman, 2017

Text copyright © Franklin Watts, 2017

Produced under licence from Battersea Dogs Home Ltd.
Battersea Dogs & Cats Home

Royalties from the sale of this book go towards supporting the
work of Battersea Dogs & Cats Home (Registered charity no 206394)
battersea.org.uk

Credits
Editor: Sarah Peutrill
Design: Sophie Pelham
Cover design: Peter Scoulding

The Author and Publisher would like to thank the staff of
Battersea Dogs & Cats Home for their guidance with this book.

ISBN: 978 1445 5067 3

Printed in China

Franklin Watts
An imprint of
Hachette Children's Group
Part of The Watts Publishing Group
Carmelite House
50 Victoria Embankment
London EC4Y 0DZ

An Hachette UK Company
www.hachette.co.uk
www.franklinwatts.co.uk

FSC
www.fsc.org
MIX
Paper from
responsible sources
FSC® C104740

I ♥ dogs

Good bye!

by Alex

Pic credits: Africa
Studio/Shutterstock: 32c. Alias
Studiot Oy/Shutterstock: 13br. Maksym Azovtsev /
Shutterstock: 7tl, 28tr. Capture Light/Shutterstock: 9cr. © Battersea Dogs &
Cats Home 2017: 28tl. cynoclub/Shutterstock: 9cl. denrz/Shutterstock: 7tr. hoyou/Shutterstock:
19b, 29tl. Tony Moran/Shutterstock: 23t. Leicher Oliver/Shutterstock: 7b, 31t. Sutichak/Shutterstock: 9bl,.
I Vangelos/Shutterstock: 17b, 28br. Mr Suttipon Yakham/Shutterstock: 32b. Every attempt has been made to clear copyright.
Should there be any inadvertent omission please apply to the publisher for rectification.